Celebrating the Twelve Days of Christmas

Celebrating the Twelve Days of Christmas

A Family Devotional in the Eastern Orthodox Tradition

AmandaEve Wigglesworth
Designed and illustrated by Grace Brooks

Conciliar Press • Chesterton, Indiana

Celebrating the Twelve Days of Christmas
A Family Devotional in the Eastern Orthodox Tradition

Unless otherwise noted, all Scripture quotations are from the New King James Version of the Bible, © 1979,1980,1982,1984 by Thomas Nelson, Inc., Nashville, Tennessee, and are used by permission.

Published by   Conciliar Press
                A division of Conciliar Media Ministries
                P.O. Box 748
                Chesterton, IN 46304

Printed in the United States of America

ISBN: 978-1-936270-54-5

Library of Congress Cataloging-in-Publication Data

Wigglesworth, Amanda Eve, 1980-
Celebrating the twelve days of Christmas : a family devotional in the
Eastern Orthodox tradition / Amanda Eve Wigglesworth ; designed and
illustrated by Grace Brooks.
    p. cm.
ISBN 978-1-936270-54-5 (alk. paper)
1. Christmas. 2. Families--Religious life. 3. Orthodox Eastern
Church--Doctrines. I. Brooks, Grace, 1960- II. Title.
BV45.W533 2012
263'.915--dc23
                        2012030538

Table of Contents

*To Jaime René, for the inspiration —
and to Kevin, for your support.*

Introduction

What Are the Twelve Days of Christmas?

After forty days of fasting and preparing for Christmas, we now begin the season of feasting! We begin celebrating on Christmas Day, and then keep celebrating for twelve more days until we reach the Feast of Theophany.

The Twelve Musical Days of Christmas

There is a popular Christmas song called "The Twelve Days of Christmas" in which a suitor gives presents each day to his true love. This song was written during a time when people would exchange one small gift a day throughout all twelve days. This led up to the final day, when they held a Twelfth Night party with a big meal, after which they would perform little plays for one another.

While the song is usually seen as a nonsense song, we can also use it to remind ourselves of the gifts God gives us. In fact, some people suggest the song was originally written by Christians in sixteenth-century England during the religious wars, in order to teach their children their faith in a secretive way. However, this is only a theory, and the origins of the song are unclear. It is always good to be reminded of God in everything around us, so in each devotional, we will look at the Christian meanings given to the gifts in this popular song.

Traditions

Christmas traditions vary from one culture to another and from one home to another. Many of the traditions surrounding the twelve days of Christmas have been lost—to the point where many people do not know these days were even celebrated, or they believe the twelve days occur before Christmas.

Some activities are provided in this book as suggestions for your family. They can help you celebrate the twelve days of Christmas together. In the first section, you will find activities for the whole season, such as creating a Twelve Days of Christmas mobile.

In the main section of the book, you will find a couple of pages devoted to each day. Each of these includes the troparion and kontakion (variable hymns) for the day, a reflection on the main event or saint remembered on that day, a Christian interpretation of the symbolism in the folk song "The Twelve Days of Christmas," and a family activity. (Dates are given according to the "new" or Gregorian calendar first, followed by the date according to the "old" or Julian calendar.)

In the last section, we have provided additional craft ideas, recipes, and so forth. You can also be creative and come up with new traditions for your family.

Activities for the Whole Season

You will most likely want to pick and choose, and adapt the following activities to suit your family's needs. Be creative!

Gift-Giving

One traditional way to celebrate the twelve days of Christmas is to give one small gift each day of the feast. This may be difficult to introduce to children who are accustomed to opening all their gifts at once, so here are a few suggestions:

- **Spread it out:** Children can open one gift on Christmas, then one gift on each day of the post-feast.
- **Stocking Stuffers:** Wrap 12 presents and put them in a stocking. Children can open their large presents on Christmas itself and then open one little package from their stocking each day of the post-feast.
- **Candy and Sweets:** Pick a designated candy or sweet. Children can receive one or two pieces each day.
- **My Favorite Things:** Secretively gather some of the children's toys or other possessions and wrap them up. Children can then choose one item per day and see what you've taken.

Christmas Wreath

Create a wreath with one large white candle in the center (representing Christ) and twelve smaller white candles in a circle. Light the large Christ-candle on Christmas Day, then light one additional candle on each following day. You may wish to have family members take turns lighting the candles.

Create a Twelve Days of Christmas Mobile/Tree

Using the song, "The Twelve Days of Christmas," cut and color appropriate pictures that match the verse of the day. Display the pictures on a poster board or on your Christmas tree, or create a mobile.

Yule Log

If you have a fireplace in your home, you may want to burn a Yule log each night from Christmas until Theophany. This was a popular tradition in Great Britain. It is also possible to find a Yule log program on the television, so even if you don't have a fireplace, you can still enjoy a Yuletide fire.

The
Twelve Days
of Christmas

Christmas

DAY

Christ is Born! Glorify Him!

This is how we greet one another during the Christmas feast. Through these words, we are announcing three things about Jesus.

First, we are saying that Jesus is the Christ. The Greek word *Christos* means "anointed one." This word means the same thing as the Hebrew word *Messiah*. A long time ago, God had promised to send a Messiah to Israel. The people of Israel were waiting with great anticipation for this Messiah. Jesus is this Messiah!

When we say that Jesus is the Christ, we are announcing to the world that He is the long-awaited Savior.

December 25/ January 7

Secondly, we are announcing that He is born. We say this part with excitement! Imagine if you were one of the Israelites waiting impatiently for the Messiah to come. Wouldn't you be excited to know that He had been born? Announcing that Christ is born is an important part of our faith. We are saying that we believe God Himself became like us as a little child

Troparion (Tone 4)

Your Nativity, O Christ our God,

Has shone to the world the light of wisdom.

For by it, those who worshiped the stars

Were taught by a star to adore You,

The Sun of Righteousness,

And to know You, the Orient from on high.

O Lord, glory to You!

Kontakion (Tone 4)

Today the Virgin gives birth to the Transcendent One

And the earth offers a cave to the Unapproachable One.

Angels with shepherds glorify Him.

The wise men journey with a star,

Since for our sake the eternal God was born as a little child!

14

and was born, just like every other human being. It can be difficult to believe that God humbled Himself enough to be born like us, but we truly believe that Jesus is one hundred percent God *and* one hundred percent human.

Third, we give a command: "Glorify Him!" We glorify Christ by praising, worshipping, and obeying Him. When we tell each other to glorify Jesus, the baby who was just born, we are reminded that He is God and that God chose to be born as a man for us.

How strange it is to think that God Himself could be born! This is the great mystery of Christmas: that the God of all creation could humble Himself and be born as a little baby.

Christ is Born! Glorify Him!

Caroling

Invite others from your parish or neighborhood to join your family in caroling, either in the community or at a hospital, care home, or other facility. (Be sure to call ahead to arrange a time to visit these facilities.) Or just gather some people together and have a sing-along at your home.

After singing, serve hot spiced cider, Christmas cookies, and popcorn.

THE *first* DAY OF CHRISTMAS

December 26/
January 8

ON THE DAY AFTER CHRISTMAS we remember Mary, Christ's moth r. She is a very important part of the Christmas story. She agreed to become pregnant with Jesus even though she wasn't married yet. She carried Him inside her for nine months, nourishing Him so He would grow. She gave birth to Him in a stable where the animals lived. And after His birth, she nursed Him, changed His diapers, and raised Him just as every mother raises her babies. We are thankful that Mary was so humble. We are thankful that Mary agreed to become His mother!

When the angel Gabriel came to her and told her God's plan, she agreed simply by saying, "Behold the maid-servant of the Lord! Let it be to me according to your word" (Luke 1:38). Her response to Gabriel should encourage us to accept God's plan for our lives and to live obediently by following His commands.

Kontakion (Tone 6)

He who before the morning star
Was begotten, without mother, of the father,
Is today, without father, made flesh upon earth of you.
A star announces the good tidings to the magi
While angels with shepherds sing the praises of your undefiled child-bearing,
O Theotokos, full of grace!

Most Holy Theotokos, save us!

*On the first day of
Christmas,
my true love
gave to me* 1 *a partridge in
a pear tree*

The "true love" in this song is God, who gives gifts to all of us. This song explains twelve of those gifts—one for each day. Today, on the first day of Christmas, we are given the symbol of a partridge in a pear tree. This represents Christ, who is shown as a bird in a tree. The image of the bird reminds us of His sadness over Jerusalem when He compared Himself to a mother hen: *"O Jerusalem, Jerusalem, the one who kills the prophets and stones those who are sent to her! How often I wanted to gather your children together, as a hen gathers her brood under her wings, but you were not willing!"* (Luke 13:34). The pear tree reminds us that Jesus is the tree of life.

Family Time

Many people go shopping or return unwanted gifts to stores on December 26. Counteract the hustle and bustle of holiday shopping by staying home and playing games together as a family. If you have received gifts you can't use, plan to pass them on to someone who could use them.

THE second DAY OF CHRISTMAS

St. Stephen the Protomartyr

December 27/ January 9

AFTER CELEBRATING Christ's birth and remembering His mother, the Church begins to remember those who were martyred for Christ. The Greek word for martyr (*martyrios*) means "a witness." The martyrs are remembered as saints not just because they died, but because they confessed their belief that Christ is God, even when people did cruel things to them to try to make them deny that belief. They were eventually killed because they refused to deny Christ.

The first person to be martyred after Christ's death, resurrection, and ascension was Stephen. His speech declaring his faith in Christ is recorded in the Acts of the Apostles (Acts 6:8—8:2). By remembering Stephen's confession and martyrdom, we remind ourselves that Christmas is about more than just the birth of a baby. This baby forces us to decide whether we will follow Him each and every day, or deny Him and follow our own desires.

SAINT STEPHEN

Holy Protomartyr Stephen, pray for us!

Troparion (Tone 4)

O Protomartyr and mighty warrior of Christ our God,

You are victorious in battle and crowned with glory, O holy Stephen!

You confounded the council of your persecutors,

Beholding your Savior enthroned at the right hand of the Father.

Never cease to intercede for the salvation of our souls!

Kontakion (Tone 3)

Yesterday, the Master assumed our flesh and became our guest;

Today, His servant is stoned to death and departs in the flesh:

The glorious Protomartyr Stephen.

***On the second day
of Christmas,
my true love
gave to me*** 2 *turtle doves …*

The number two represents the two covenants: the Old Testament and the New Testament. The number two also reminds us that Christ is both God and man. This teaching is often called "the two natures of Christ."

Giving

Have each member of the family select a present that he or she just received. Take these gifts and edible goodies (these could be from your stash of Christmas baking) and give them to a family in need. For some people, giving up a present may seem like a small martyrdom. Instead, may this activity remind you of all the blessings you have.

THE *third* DAY OF CHRISTMAS

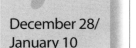

December 28/
January 10

AT THE BEGINNING of the fourth century, the emperor Maximian (284–305) gave orders to destroy Christian churches, to burn service books, and to deprive all Christians of the rights and privileges of citizenship.

On the Feast of the Nativity of Christ in the year 302, approximately 20,000 Christians had assembled at the cathedral in Nicomedia when a messenger from the emperor arrived at the church. He told the Christians that soldiers were surrounding the building and were planning to set it on fire. Anyone who wished to leave the church was free to leave, but had to offer sacrifice to the pagan gods.

Not one person chose to leave the church! As the soldiers prepared to set fire to the church, Bishop Anthimus baptized all the catechumens and gave communion to everyone. All 20,000 of the Christians died in the fire except Bishop Anthimus, who managed to escape. The emperor Maximian thought he had killed all the Christians of Nicomedia, but he was wrong. There was at least one Christian left in Nicomedia that day.

Then, as He was now drawing near the descent of the Mount of Olives, the whole multitude of the disciples began to rejoice and praise God with a loud voice for all the mighty works they had seen, saying:

"'Blessed is the King who comes in the name of the Lord!' Peace in heaven and glory in the highest!"

And some of the Pharisees called to Him from the crowd, "Teacher, rebuke Your disciples."

Troparion (Tone 2)

Blessed is the earth that received your blood, passion-bearers of the Lord,

And holy is the dwelling place which received your spirits.

You triumphed over the enemy in the stadium

And you preached Christ with boldness.

Since He is good, we pray that you beseech Him to save our souls.

Kontakion (Tone 1)

Their souls strengthened by faith,

The twenty thousand martyrs accepted their suffering by fire

And cried out to You, the One born of the Virgin:

"Like gold, myrrh, and frankincense, the gifts of the Persian kings,

Receive our whole burnt offering, O Eternal God."

But He answered and said to them, "I tell you that if these should keep silent, the stones would immediately cry out." (Luke 19:37–40)

On the third day of Christmas, my true love gave to me

French hens ...

The number three reminds us of the Holy Trinity: Father, Son, and Holy Spirit.

What to Do

Take the story of the martyrs of Nicomedia, or a favorite Bible story connected with Christmas, and act it out with simple props and costumes. Invite grandparents & friends to watch.

Suggested stories:
- *Daniel in the Lion's Den*
- *The Three Holy Youths*
- *The Annunciation*
- *The Nativity story*

THE *fourth* DAY OF CHRISTMAS

YESTERDAY AND THE DAY BEFORE, we remembered saints who chose to honor Christ. Today, we remember the Holy Innocents, who did not have a choice.

When the Magi from the East followed a star to Judea, they visited King Herod first. The King ordered them to come back after they had found the Child so that he could go worship Him too. However, he did not plan on worshipping Christ.

The Magi were warned in a dream not to return to King Herod, so they returned to their homeland another way. When King Herod realized that his plan to find and kill the Child would not be successful, he ordered his army to kill all the male children two years old and younger near Bethlehem.

Herod thought that Jesus would be among the dead children, but He was not killed because Joseph had been warned in a dream to take Mary and Jesus to Egypt. They remained there until King Herod died, and then they returned home to Galilee.

December 29/ January 11

Troparion (Tone 1)

We beseech You, O Lord of mankind,

To accept in supplication

The suffering which Your saints endured for Your sake, O Lord,

And to heal all our infirmities.

Kontakion (Tone 8)

When the King was born in Bethlehem, the Magi came from the East.

Having been led by a star from on High, they brought Him gifts.

But in exceeding wrath, Herod harvested the infants as sorrowing wheat;

The rule of his kingdom has come to an end.

O Holy Innocents, pray for us!

*On the fourth day
of Christmas,
my true love gave
to me*

4

calling birds …

The number four
represents the
four Gospels:
Matthew, Mark,
Luke, and John.

Holy Innocents' Wreath

Choose one small white candle for each child in the home (or, for each person in the home). Arrange the candles in a wreath, or in candlesticks arranged as you like. Have the youngest child light the candles (with help if necessary).

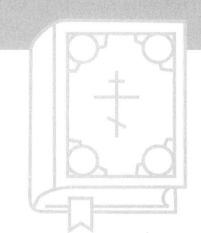

THE *fifth* DAY OF CHRISTMAS

THE MARTYR ANYSIA lived in the city of Thessalonica during the reign of the emperor Maximian (284–305). After her parents died, she sold everything she owned, gave her riches to the poor, and led a strict life of fasting and prayer.

December 30/
January 12

We learned on December 28 (Jan. 10) that Maximian persecuted Christians. He even made a law that said anyone could kill a Christian and would not be punished for it. It was dangerous to admit you were a Christian because anyone could kill you.

One day, when St. Anysia was going to church, a soldier stopped her on the road and tried to take her to a pagan festival to offer sacrifices to the Roman gods. She refused, gently moving away from him. When he forcefully grabbed her, she pushed him away, spat in his face, and said, "My Lord Jesus Christ forbids you!" The soldier became angry and killed her with his sword.

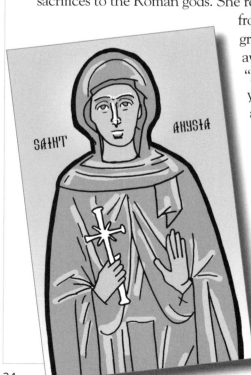

SAINT ANYSIA

Christians came and took her body and buried it near the city gates. Later on, a chapel was built over her grave. St. Anysia's example challenges us to be faithful to Christ when it is not easy.

O Virgin-Martyr Anysia, pray for us!

Troparion (Tone 4)

Your lamb Anysia, O Jesus,
Calls out to You in a loud voice:
"I love You, O my Bridegroom,
And in seeking You, I endure suffering.
In Baptism, I was crucified so that I might reign in You,
And died so that I might live with You.
Accept me as a pure sacrifice,
For I have offered myself in love."
By her prayers, save our souls since You are merciful.

Kontakion (Tone 4)

Like a lamp with two flames,
You illumine Christ's Church with mystical radiance.
In your martyr's contest, you brought forth fruits a hundredfold, O Anysia;
And you, O Melania, were resplendent in asceticism.
You were found worthy of the incorruptible life of the blessed!

*On the fifth day
of Christmas,
my true love gave to me*

gold rings ...

Thank-You Cards

Make and write thank-you cards for the gifts you have received. You might cut pictures from the Christmas cards you received or make paper snowflakes to decorate your cards. Construction paper, puff paint, and glitter glue are useful too.

The number five reminds us of the first five books of the Bible: Genesis, Exodus, Leviticus, Numbers, and Deuteronomy. These five books are a very important part of the Jewish Scriptures and have many names: the Pentateuch, the Torah, the Law, and the Books of Moses.

THE *sixth* DAY OF CHRISTMAS

SAINT MELANIA was born in Rome into a wealthy Christian family. Melania desired to live as a monastic, but her parents arranged for her to marry when she was fourteen years old. After her son and daughter both died as young children, her husband agreed that they should live as monastics.

December 31/
January 13

Melania and her husband left Rome and gave their lives completely to serving God. They visited sick people, helped travelers, sold their properties, and used their money to help monasteries, hospitals, churches, widows, and orphans in many countries. After giving away all their money to help others, they spent their days in poverty and prayer, and rarely saw each other because they lived in different monasteries.

Melania started a monastery that grew quickly to ninety women. Later, she wanted to build a monastery for men on the Mount of the Ascension. Someone gave a large donation of money so that she could do this, and the monastery was built in a single year.

At that time, some people were teaching things about Christ that did not agree with what the Church believes. Melania was one person who taught people the true Orthodox teachings.

SAINT MELANIA

Troparion (Tone 4)

In your fervent desire for the angelic life,
You renounced the comforts of this earth.
In watchfulness, you practiced sobriety and deep humility.
Therefore, most wise Melania, you became a pure vessel
Filled by the Holy Spirit, who adorned you with gifts,
Attracting all to your divine fervor,
Leading them to the Master and Savior of our souls.

Kontakion (Tone 4)

Your soul radiated light from the One born for us of the Virgin,
And you shone with virtues, O saint worthy of all praise.
By giving away your possessions on earth,
You stored up treasures in Heaven,
Showing a wonderful example of the ascetic life.
Therefore, O holy Melania, we honor you with love.

At the end of her life, she sensed it was her time to leave this world, and she told the priest and other nuns. They were very sad to hear she would be leaving them. She peacefully joined the Lord in the year 439. This holy lady gives us a good example of how we can follow the Lord's command to sell all our possessions and give everything to the poor.

Holy Mother Melania, pray for us!

On the sixth day of Christmas, my true love gave to me

geese a-laying …

Visiting

Following St. Melania's example, visit someone in need (i.e. a widow, orphan, someone who is sick, someone in the hospital) or help a traveler.

The number six reminds us of the six days of creation.

THE Seventh DAY OF CHRISTMAS

The Circumcision of Christ/St. Basil the Great/St. Emilia the mother of Basil

WHEN A JEWISH BOY IS BORN, he is circumcised on the eighth day after his birth. In obedience to His own law, our Lord was circumcised on the eighth day. The Church Fathers explain that Christ chose to be circumcised for at least two reasons: first, to give people an example of faithful obedience, and second, so that no one would doubt that He had really come in the flesh. Christians are no longer required to be circumcised, but we are still called to circumcise our hearts (Deut. 10:16). This means we choose to follow God, and we set ourselves apart for His service and worship alone.

■ ■ ■

January 2/ January 15

SAINT BASIL THE GREAT, Archbishop of Caesarea in Cappadocia, was born in 330 at Caesarea. He was brilliant and studied many subjects. He was a teacher of the Orthodox faith in the face of false teachings and wrote many works to help explain the faith. He also wrote certain prayers which we still pray today, and arranged the prayers and hymns in the St. Basil's Liturgy, which is usually celebrated on Holy Saturday and Christmas Eve as well as during Great Lent. He was loved by all in the Church for his deep knowledge of Scripture, his desire for peace and unity, and his care for those in need. St. Basil labored for the Church until his death on January 1, 379, at age 49.

Troparion (Tone 4)

You were revealed as the sure foundation of the Church,

Granting all mankind a lordship which cannot be taken away,

Sealing it with your precepts,

Venerable Basil, revealer of heaven.

Troparion (Tone 1)

Enthroned on high with the Eternal Father and Your divine Spirit,

O Jesus, You willed to be born on earth of the unwedded handmaid, Your Mother.

Therefore, You were circumcised as an eight-day old Child.

Glory to Your most gracious counsel;

Glory to Your dispensation;

Glory to Your condescension, O only Lover of mankind.

Kontakion (Tone 3)

The Lord of all accepts to be circumcised.

Thus, as He is good, He excises the sins of mortal men.

Today, He grants the world salvation,

While light-bearing Basil, high priest of our Creator,

Rejoices in heaven as a divine initiate of Christ.

SAINT BASIL THE GREAT

Saints Basil and Emilia, pray for us!

On the seventh day of Christmas, my true love gave to me

7

swans a-swimming …

A Restful New Year's Day

On the seventh day of Christmas, enjoy a day of rest. Choose a family activity that is restful and enjoyable for your family.

Greek Orthodox traditionally celebrate this day with a special St. Basil's cake. A coin is baked into the cake, and the person who finds it will be especially blessed in the coming year. (See page 40 for a recipe.)

The number seven reminds us of the seventh day of creation, when God rested. It is considered to be a number of wholeness and perfection, and the number of God. It can also remind us of the seven gifts of the Holy Spirit: prophecy, ministry, teaching, exhortation, giving, leadership, and compassion (Rom. 12:6–8; 1 Cor. 12:8–11)

THE eighth DAY OF CHRISTMAS

SAINT SERAPHIM OF SAROV,

a well-loved saint of the Russian Church, was born on July 19, 1754. From his early childhood, he loved God and loved to attend church services. When he was still quite young, he became a monk. The Lord blessed him with visions of the Theotokos, the angels, and St. John the Theologian. He was saved from death many times: once when he fell from a high place, once when he was very sick, and again when robbers came and beat him up.

After many years of living in a monastery, he went deep into the forest to live as a hermit. St. Seraphim read the Scriptures, the services, and the writings of the Church Fathers. He knew many hymns by heart and would sing them while he worked in the forest. He kept a small garden and fasted a lot. He did not receive visitors because he did not want to be disturbed in his prayers. His only visitors were the animals of the forest. He was so calm and peaceful in his spirit that the animals would come and eat out of his hand, even the bears. St. Seraphim once said, "Acquire the spirit of peace, and a thousand souls around you will be saved."

January 2/
January 15

SAINT SERAPHIM

Troparion (Tone 4)

By your righteous deeds, you revealed to the world

An image of the perfect servant of the Lord.

By your fasting, vigil, and prayers, You were inspired in your evangelical life,

Feeding the hungry and caring for the poor,

Nursing the sick and strengthening the weak.

Now you stand at the right hand of the Master, Christ,

O holy Juliana, interceding for our souls.

Kontakion (Tone 2)

Forsaking the beauty as well as the corruption of this world,

You settled in the monastery of Sarov, O Saint.

There, you lived an angelic life,

Becoming for many the way to salvation.

Therefore, Christ has glorified you, Father Seraphim,

Enriching you with abundant healing and miracles.

So we cry to you: "Save us by your prayers, venerable Seraphim, our father."

Later in his life, he received another vision of the Theotokos, who instructed him to stop being a hermit and to open his door to pilgrims. In this way, he was able to bless and heal people around him and teach them how to follow Christ by his own example. St. Seraphim fell asleep in the Lord kneeling in front of an icon of the Theotokos on January 2, 1833.

Saint Seraphim, pray for us!

On the fifth day of Christmas, my true love gave to me

maids a-milking ...

Art Project

Find a picture book that tells the story of Noah's Ark and read it together. See how many animals you can name that would have been in the ark and draw pictures of them. (Don't forget St. Seraphim's bears!) You could mount your colored pictures on cardstock and make a mobile.

The number eight reminds us of the eight people saved in the ark, and also of the eight Beatitudes (which we sing during the Third Antiphon of the Divine Liturgy).

THE *ninth* DAY OF CHRISTMAS

THE PROPHET

Malachi was the last Old Testament prophet. He lived 400 years before the Birth of Christ, when the Jews had returned to Israel after being captives in Babylon. In his prophetic book, he prophesies about the coming of Jesus Christ and His Forerunner (Mal. 3:1–5; 4:1–6).

■ ■ ■

January 3/ January 16

SAINT GENEVIEVE

was born in Gaul (modern France) in the village of Nanterre, near Paris, around 422. When she was about seven years old, St. Germanus of Auxerre noticed her as he was passing through Nanterre. The bishop kissed her on the head and told her parents she would become great in the sight of God and would lead many to salvation.

When it was reported that Attila the Hun was approaching Paris, Genevieve and the nuns of Nanterre fasted and prayed that God would spare the city of Paris. Suddenly, the attacking troops turned away from Paris and went off in another direction.

Years later, when she was fifteen, Genevieve was taken to Paris to enter the monastic life. Through fasting, vigil, and prayer, she progressed in monasticism and received from God the gifts of

Troparion (Tone 2)

The memory of Your prophet Malachi

We do celebrate this day, O Lord.

By his prayers we beseech You,

O Christ God, to save our souls.

Kontakion (Tone 4)

Endowed with the gift of prophecy, O Malachi,

You proclaimed clearly the saving coming of Christ to the world.

His brightness has brought light to the whole universe!

Holy Prophet Malachi, pray for us!

seeing the future and of working miracles. Gradually, the people of Paris and the surrounding area came to regard Genevieve as a holy person.

One night, she was on her way to church with her nuns when the wind blew out her lantern. The nuns could not find their way without a light, since it was dark and stormy, and the road was rough and muddy. St. Genevieve made the sign of the cross over the lantern, and the candle lit with a bright flame. St. Genevieve fell asleep in the Lord around 512 at the age of eighty-nine.

Saint Genevieve, pray for us!

On the ninth day of Christmas, my true love gave to me

ladies dancing …

Luminarias

Make and/or decorate candles or luminarias as a reminder of St. Genevieve's lantern. See page 43 for instructions on making luminarias.

The number nine reminds us that Christ died at the ninth hour. This is the same time that we call three P.M. The number nine can also remind us of the nine fruits of the Holy Spirit: love, joy, peace, patience, kindness, generosity, faithfulness, gentleness, and self-control (Galatians 5:22).

THE *tenth* DAY OF CHRISTMAS

THE LORD JESUS CHRIST sent the Seventy Apostles to go before Him two by two into the cities He would visit (Luke 10:1). They were present at Pentecost and went as missionaries to proclaim the good news of salvation. Many of them were put in prison and killed because of their faith in Christ. Among them, Mark, Luke, James, Timothy, Titus, and Philemon are familiar to us because Mark and Luke each wrote a Gospel, James wrote an epistle, and Timothy, Titus, and Philemon each received an epistle from Paul. All of these writings are in the New Testament. (For a complete list of the Seventy Apostles, see page 41.)

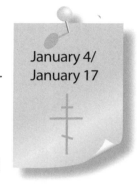

January 4/
January 17

Troparion (Tone 3)

Holy apostles of the Seventy,
Entreat the merciful God
To grant our souls forgiveness
of transgressions.

Kontakion (Tone 2)

O faithful, let us praise with hymns
The choir of the seventy disciples of Christ.
They have taught us all to worship the undivided Trinity,
For they are divine lamps of the Faith.

O Holy
Apostles,
pray for us!

MARK was born in Jerusalem. He lived close to the Garden of Gethsemane and was in the garden when Jesus was arrested. After the Ascension, Mark traveled with Paul and Peter to various places. Then he went to Egypt and started churches there. Mark was the first person to write a Gospel. He composed a liturgy for the Christians in Alexandria and also started a Christian school there. Many important Church Fathers from Egypt went to this school.

LUKE was born in Syrian Antioch, a city outside of Palestine. He was a doctor trained in Greek medicine. When he heard about Jesus, he traveled to Palestine, accepted the Lord's teaching, and became one of the seventy apostles.

After the Ascension, Luke traveled with Paul until Paul's death. Luke wrote a Gospel as well as the Acts of the Apostles while he was in Rome with Paul. Tradition tells us that Luke painted the first icons of the Theotokos.

JAMES, the brother of Jesus, became the first bishop of Jerusalem. He was an important leader in the early Church. He wrote a letter addressed to the Jews who were scattered around the Roman Empire. Christians loved him, but the Jews did not want him to preach about Christ. One day, a group of people threw him off of the Temple roof because he was preaching about Christ.

*On the tenth day
of Christmas,
my true love gave to me*

10

lords a-leaping ...

Stained Glass Project

Pick one of the icons available at www.conciliarpress. com/12-days-icons or another coloring picture and make a stained glass picture. See instructions on page 42.

The number ten reminds us of the Ten Commandments.

THE eleventh DAY OF CHRISTMAS

TODAY IS A DAY OF STRICT FASTING as we prepare for the great feast of Theophany beginning this evening. A special service is normally served after Vespers called the Blessing of the Waters. At this service, we celebrate the Lord's baptism and bless large amounts of water. After the water is blessed, the priest uses it to bless the whole church. At the veneration of the cross, the people come forward to drink some of the water. People can take this water home and use it to bless their homes by sprinkling it, and to bless themselves by drinking it.

January 5/ January 18

What is so special about this water? Water is very important for humans. We need to drink water in order to live. Water is an important image in the Bible that reminds us God is the one who gives us life. He is the water of life. If we drink of Him, we will not be thirsty for spiritual life because we will be satisfied.

We also use water to clean things, and to clean ourselves. The waters of baptism make us clean on the outside, which represents how Christ washes us clean of our sins on the inside. The water blessed at Theophany is extra special because the Holy Spirit blesses it, and because every time we celebrate the Lord's baptism we remember our own baptism.

Troparion (Tone 4)

Of old, the river Jordan
Turned back before
Elisha's mantle at Elijah's
ascension.

The waters were parted in two
And the waterway became a dry path.

This is truly a symbol of baptism
By which we pass through this mortal life.

Christ has appeared in the Jordan to sanctify the waters!

Kontakion (Tone 4)

Today, the Lord enters the Jordan and cries out to John:
"Do not be afraid to baptize Me.
For I have come to save Adam, the first-formed man."

Christ is baptized in the River Jordan! Glorify Him!

*On the eleventh day
of Christmas,
my true love gave to me*

11 *pipers piping ...*

What to Do

See how many different uses of water you can think of. One of them is cleaning—this might be the day you clean your home in preparation for a party or house-blessing. Have everyone pitch in!

Remember to bring a container to church so you can bring some holy water home with you.

The number eleven reminds us of the eleven faithful disciples.

THE twelfth DAY OF CHRISTMAS

AT THEOPHANY, we celebrate the time when all three Persons of the Trinity were evident to human eyes and ears. At Christ's Baptism, we hear the voice of God the Father, we see God the Son in the river, and we see God the Holy Spirit taking the form of a dove. Christ did not need to be baptized in order to be forgiven—He is God and never sinned. However, Christ was baptized in order to be obedient, to fulfill the Law, to reveal the mystery of the Trinity, to give us the example of baptism, and as a symbol of His death and Resurrection, which were going to happen later on in His ministry. He also sanctified all the water in the world when He entered the waters of the Jordan.

January 6/
January 19

The feast of Theophany has always been a very important feast for Orthodox Christians. In the early Church, this feast was even more important

Troparion (Tone 1)

When You, O Lord, were baptized in the Jordan,

The worship of the Trinity was made manifest,

For the voice of the Father bore witness to You,

And called You His beloved Son.

And the Spirit, in the form of a dove,

Confirmed the truthfulness of His word.

O Christ our God, who have revealed Yourself

And have enlightened the world, glory to You!

Kontakion (Tone 4)

Today, You have appeared to the whole universe,

And Your light, O Lord, has shone on us

Who with understanding praise You.

You have come and revealed Yourself,

O unapproachable Light.

than the celebration of Christ's birth. After a while, both the birth and baptism of Christ were celebrated on the same day. Later on, the feast was separated into two feasts: Christmas on December 25, with twelve days of Christmas to celebrate until Theophany on January 6.

Christ is baptized in the River Jordan! Glorify Him!

On the twelfth day of Christmas, my true love gave to me

drummers drumming …

Twelfth Night Party

Have a social event on the Twelfth Night, or sometime during the post-feast. You could play games, have a talent show, sing songs, have the children perform skits, enjoy a meal together, and enjoy yummy holiday treats.

The number twelve reminds us of the twelve apostles, the twelve tribes of Israel, and the twelve great feasts of the church year.

Vasilopita (St. Basil's Cake)

Many recipes for this traditional New Year's cake are available from cookbooks, websites, and *yiayias* everywhere (*yiayia* is Greek for grandma). Since this recipe does not use yeast, young cooks do not need to wait for the dough to rise. This cake is light (like a torte). You can also find heavier recipes if you want your vasilopita to be more like a pound cake.

Ingredients

1 c. Butter

2 t. Orange or lemon rind

1 T. Lemon juice

1-3/4 c. Sugar

5 Eggs

2 c. Flour

2 t. Baking powder

½ t. Baking soda

¼ t. Cinnamon

1 c. Milk

¼ c. Walnuts and/or pistachios

¼ c. Slivered almonds

1 coin, sterilized or wrapped in foil

1 Egg white

¼ c. Sesame seeds

½ c. Whole almonds (enough to form a cross on the top)

¼ c. Honey, warmed

¼ c. Confectioner's sugar

Preparation

1. Preheat oven to 350° F.
2. In a large bowl, cream softened butter, lemon/orange rind, lemon juice, and sugar with an electric mixer until light and fluffy.
3. Beat in eggs, one at a time.
4. Beat in flour, baking powder, baking soda, and cinnamon.
5. Beat in milk, a little at a time.
6. Add nuts and mix until combined.
7. Grease two 9" inch round cake pans really well. Pour the batter into the prepared pans.
9. Slide the coin into the batter and smooth over the top.
10. Bake for 20 minutes.
11. Remove one cake from oven. Brush the top with egg white. Sprinkle sesame seeds over the top. Place almonds in the shape of a cross and press into the cake slightly.
12. Return the cake to the oven and bake for another 10–15 minutes until both cakes are golden and cooked thoroughly.
13. Let the cakes stand in the pan for 5–10 minutes, then turn out onto a cooling rack, being careful not to let the topping fall off.
14. Cool completely.
15. Place the undecorated cake on a plate. Drizzle the top with warm honey. Stack the decorated cake on top. Sprinkle with confectioner's sugar before serving.

The Seventy Disciples of the Lord

1. James the Brother of the Lord (October 23)
2. Mark the Evangelist (April 25)
3. Luke the Evangelist (October 18)
4. Cleopas, brother of St. Joseph the Betrothed (October 30)
5. Simeon (April 27)
6. Barnabas (June 11)
7. Joses, called Barsabas (October 30)
8. Thaddeus (August 21)
9. Ananias (October 1)
10. Protomartyr Stephen the Archdeacon (December 27)
11. Philip the Deacon (October 11)
12. Prochorus the Deacon (July 28)
13. Nicanor the Deacon (July 28 and December 28)
14. Timon the Deacon (July 28 and December 30)
15. Parmenas the Deacon (July 28)
16. Timothy (January 22)
17. Titus (August 25)
18. Philemon (November 22 and February 19)
19. Onesimus (February 15)
20. Epaphras (November 22 and February 19)
21. Archippus (November 22 and February 19)
22. Silas (July 30)
23. Silvanus (July 30)
24. Crescens (July 30)
25. Crispus (July 30)
26. Epaenetos (July 30)
27. Andronicus (May 17 and July 30)
28. Stachys (October 31)
29. Amplias (October 31)
30. Urban (October 31)
31. Narcissus (October 31)
32. Apelles (October 31)
33. Aristobulus (October 31 and March 16)
34. Herodion or Rodion (April 8 and November 10)
35. Agabus (April 8)
36. Rufus (April 8)
37. Asyncritus (April 8)
38. Phlegon (April 8)
39. Hermas (November 5, November 30, and May 31)
40. Patrobas (November 5)
41. Hermes (April 8)
42. Linus (November 5)
43. Gaius (November 5)
44. Philologus (November 5)
45. Lucius (September 10)
46. Jason (April 28)
47. Sosipater (April 28 and November 10)
48. Olympas (November 10)
49. Tertius (October 30 and November 10)
50. Erastos (November 30)
51. Quartus (November 10)
52. Euodius (September 7)
53. Onesiphorus (September 7 and December 8)
54. Clement (November 25)
55. Sosthenes (December 8)
56. Apollos (March 30 and December 8)
57. Tychicus (December 8)
58. Epaphroditus (December 8)
59. Tarpus (May 26)
60. Quadratus (September 21)
61. Mark, called John (September 27)
62. Zeno (September 27)
63. Aristarchus (April 15 and September 27)
64. Pudens (April 15)
65. Trophimus (April 15)
66. Mark, nephew of Barnabas (October 30)
67. Artemas (October 30)
68. Aquila (July 14)
69. Fortunatus (June 15)
70. Achaicus (January 4)

Additional Crafts

Stained Glass Pictures

Supplies
- Coloring pages
- Wax crayons
- Cotton balls
- Cooking oil
- Ribbon/yarn
- Scissors
- Hole punch

Instructions
1. Color the right side of the picture with wax crayons.
2. Flip the page.
3. Put some cooking oil on a cotton ball and rub over the back of the picture.
4. Punch a hole at the top and attach a ribbon or piece of yarn.
5. Hang in a window or on the Christmas tree.

Christmas Tags

These can be used to decorate the windows, walls, tree, or saved to use for labeling next year's Christmas presents.

Supplies
- Old Christmas cards
- Scissors
- Ribbon/yarn
- Hole punch

Instructions
1. Cut squares or circles from old Christmas cards.
2. Punch a hole in the top and attach a ribbon.

Luminarias

Supplies
- Paper bags
- Scissors
- Tea light candles
- Sand or rocks

Instructions
1. Cut out designs in the sides of a paper bag (for example, snow-flakes, stars, or hearts).
2. Decorate the bag by coloring on it or adding glitter.
3. Fill with something heavy to weight the bag (sand, salt, rocks—anything cheap that won't burn easily)
4. Place a tea light in the bag and enjoy!

Mason Jar Luminarias

Supplies
- Glass Mason jars, any size
- Acrylic paints
- Paintbrushes
- Decorative sand
- Tea light candles

Instructions
1. Paint designs on a Mason jar.
2. Fill with decorative sand.
3. Place a tea light or votive candle in the sand and enjoy!

Tin Can Luminarias

Supplies
- Tin cans
- Water
- Marker
- Hammer
- Nail

Instructions
1. Fill the tin can with water and freeze until solid.
2. Draw a design onto the can with a marker.
3. Using a nail and hammer, punch holes in the can to create your design.
4. Let the water thaw. Drain.
5. Wash off excess marker lines.
6. Paint or decorate the tin can if you like.
7. Place a candle inside the can and enjoy!

Christmas Potpourri

Supplies
¼ c. Whole Cloves
3 oz. Cinnamon bark, broken into pieces
6 Whole nutmegs
¼ c. Allspice berries
¼ c. Dried lemon peel
¼ c. Dried orange peel

Instructions
Mix evenly. Put in sheer bags in order to place in dresser drawers. Potpourri can also be placed directly into a decorative bowl or around a candle.

The potpourri can also be used as a mulling spice. Use 2 tablespoons with 8 cups of apple or cranberry juice. Simmer on medium-low for at least 30 minutes. Parents can also use 2 tablespoons with 3 cups of red wine. Simmer on low for 30 minutes.

Toilet Paper Snowman

Supplies
• 3 rolls of toilet paper, of different sizes
• 3 sheets of white tissue paper
• Glue
• Scissors
• Decorating supplies

Instructions
1. Roll one sheet of tissue paper around one roll of toilet paper. Tuck the ends of the tissue paper into the tube. Repeat with the other two rolls.
2. Glue the rolls together so that the largest roll is on the bottom and the smallest roll is on the top.
3. Bring your snowman to life by making a nose, a mouth, two eyes, buttons, a scarf, and a hat. You can use construction paper, buttons, yarn, and any other craft supplies you have around the house.

Cardboard Angel

Supplies
Pattern (see next page)
Cardboard
Pencil
Scissors

Instructions
1. Trace pattern from page 46 onto old boxes.
2. Cut out, following the directions on page 46.
3. Decorate your angel with glitter or other decorations.
4. Slide the two body pieces together.
5. Glue the wings onto the body.

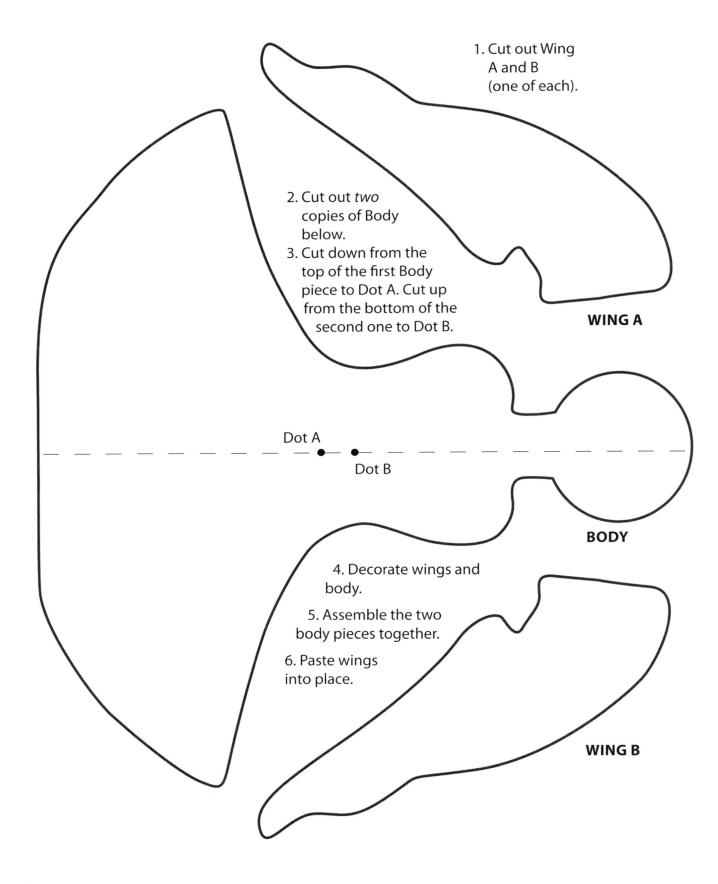

1. Cut out Wing A and B (one of each).

2. Cut out *two* copies of Body below.
3. Cut down from the top of the first Body piece to Dot A. Cut up from the bottom of the second one to Dot B.

WING A

Dot A

Dot B

BODY

4. Decorate wings and body.

5. Assemble the two body pieces together.

6. Paste wings into place.

WING B

About the Author

AMANDAEVE WIGGLESWORTH has been involved in ministry with children and youth for nineteen years. AmandaEve and her husband, Deacon Kevin, are members at St. Peter the Aleut Orthodox parish in Calgary, Alberta. She is a member of St. Peter's Camp board, where she is affectionately known as Pegesus and can very occasionally be heard singing a funky rap because a clever camper caught her putting her elbows on the table.